YOUNG DISCOVER...

BATTERIES, BULBS, AND WIRES

DAVID GLOVER

Kingfisher Books

NEW YORK

KINGFISHER
Larousse Kingfisher Chambers Inc.
95 Madison Avenue
New York, New York 10016

First American edition 1993
10 9 8 7 6 5 4 3 2 (HC)
10 9 8 7 6 5 4   (PB)
10 9 8 7 6 5 4 3 2   (LIB. BDG.)
© Grisewood & Dempsey Ltd. 1993

Library of Congress Cataloging-in-Publication
Data
Glover, David
    Batteries, bulbs, and wires / David
Glover.
        p.   cm. — (Young discoverers)
    Includes index.
    Summary: Uses activities and projects to
introduce how electricity and magnets work
at home and in the everyday world.
    1. Electricity—Juvenile literature.
2. Electricity—Experiments—Juvenile
literature. 3. Magnets—Juvenile
literature. 4. Magnets—Experiments—
Juvenile literature. [1. Electricity—
Experiments. 2. Magnets—Experiments.
3. Experiments.] I. Title. II. Series.
QC527.2.G56 1993
537'.078—dc20   92-40215 CIP AC

ISBN 1-85697-837-0 (HC)
ISBN 1-85697-933-4 (PB)
ISBN 1-85697-631-9 (LIB. BDG.)

Series editor: Sue Nicholson
Designer: Ben White
Picture research: Elaine Willis
Cover design: Dave West
Cover illustration: Kuo Kang Chen
Illustrators: Peter Bull p.26 (right); Kuo Kang Chen
    pp.2, 4, 6-7, 10, 12-25, 28-30, 31 (left);
    Chris Forsey pp.5, 8-9, 11, 26 (left), 27;
    Kevin Maddison p.31 (right)
Photographs: Taheshi Takahara/Science Photo
    Library p.24; ZEFA pp.5, 16, 22, 31

Printed in Spain

About This Book

This book tells you what magnets are, how to join batteries and wires to light up bulbs, and how electricity and magnets are linked. It also suggests lots of experiments and things to look out for. You should be able to find nearly everything you need to do the experiments around the home. You may have to buy some items, but they are all cheap and easy to find. Sometimes you will need to ask an adult to help you, such as when drilling holes.

Be a Smart Scientist

● Before you begin an experiment, read the instructions carefully and collect all the things you need.

● Put on some old clothes or wear a smock.

● When you have finished, clear everything away, especially sharp things like knives and scissors, and wash your hands.

● Keep a record of what you do and what you find out. If your results aren't quite the same as those in this book don't worry. See if you can work out what has happened, and why.

Contents

 An Electric World 4

 A First Look at Magnets 6

 Pull and Push 8

 The Pull of the Earth 10

 Magnets at Work 12

 Getting Started 14

 Simple Circuits 16

An Electric Test 18

 Three Circuit Projects 19

 Light at Night 22

 **Magnetic Links** 24

 Electric Sounds 26

 Electric Motors 28

 Making Currents 30

Index 32

An Electric World

It's hard to imagine what life was like without electricity — no electric lights, no televisions, no computers. Yet only one hundred years ago hardly any of these things existed. Scientists could make electricity with a battery or with magnets and wires, but the first electric light bulb had only just been invented. Most people still used coal and gas to heat and light their homes.

Eye-Spy

List ten things around your home that use electricity, then challenge an adult to add ten more things to your list.

In this book you'll also read about magnets. Can you think of any places where magnets are used? Perhaps you use magnets to attach messages or postcards to the door of your refrigerator.

The appliances shown below use *current* electricity. There is also a *static* electricity (see next page).

Do it yourself

Discover static electricity!

Rub a balloon against your sweater. This will make static electricity build up on the balloon's plastic skin. Then hold the balloon against a wall and remove your hand — the static electricity should make the balloon cling there.

Hint: Experiments with static electricity work best on a dry day.

Above: Electric energy is as natural as the wind and the rain. During a thunderstorm, static electricity in the clouds is released in huge flashes of lightning that light up the sky.

rub on a sweater — wool and nylon work well

WARNING!

The electric wires in your home are joined to the electricity supply from a power plant. They carry a huge amount of electricity and are very dangerous. So:
• **Never** use the main electricity supply for your experiments.
• **Never** go near electric pylons or cables like the ones in the photograph above.

5

A First Look at Magnets

Do you have any magnets? What shape are they? Magnets come in all shapes and sizes but they all pull and push with an invisible force. And all magnets pull, or attract, some things but not others. For example, all magnets attract the metal iron. So if you use a magnet to pick up pins, it will only attract them if they contain iron.

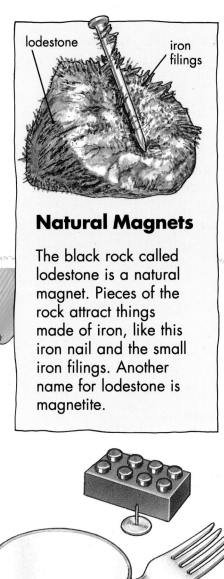

lodestone

iron filings

Natural Magnets

The black rock called lodestone is a natural magnet. Pieces of the rock attract things made of iron, like this iron nail and the small iron filings. Another name for lodestone is magnetite.

Do it yourself

Test different materials, such as nails, paper clips, pins, pencils, and coins, to see whether they are magnetic. You should be able to feel the magnet's "pull" when it attracts something.

Do it yourself

Make magnetic paper clip chains to see how strong your magnets are.

When you pick up a paper clip with a magnet, the paper clip becomes a magnet, too. You can then pick up a second paper clip on the end of the first. The stronger your magnet, the longer the chain.

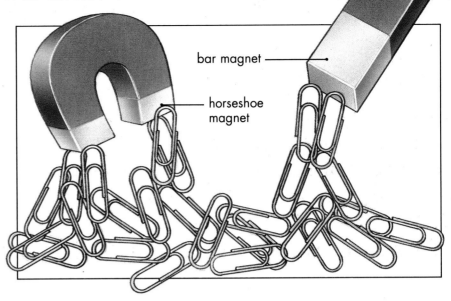

bar magnet

horseshoe magnet

See the invisible force around your magnets.

Lay a sheet of paper over a magnet and sprinkle some iron filings on top. Gently tap the paper and see how the tiny filings are pulled into a pattern around the magnet. You could try horseshoe and circular magnets, too.

If you want to keep the patterns, ask an adult to spray the paper with glue. Shake off any loose filings when dry.

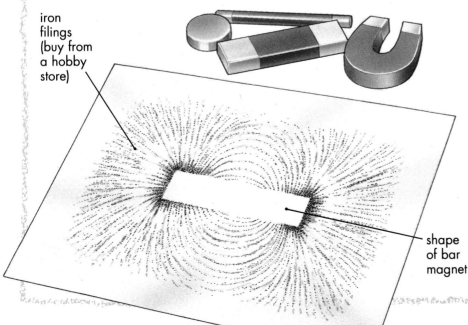

iron filings (buy from a hobby store)

shape of bar magnet

Magnet Poles

Every magnet has two poles. This is where the magnet's pulling force is strongest. Try pulling a nail away from different parts of a magnet to see how the force changes. If you cut a magnet in half, each piece would still have two poles — each half would be a complete magnet in itself.

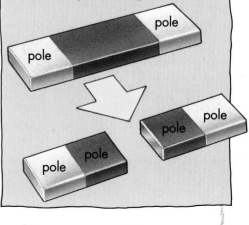

pole
pole
pole
pole
pole
pole

7

Pull and Push

The two poles of a magnet are called the north pole and the south pole. This is because when a magnet swings freely it always settles with its north pole pointing toward Earth's North Pole, and its south pole pointing south. Both poles of a magnet attract iron, but the poles of different magnets do not always attract or pull toward each other. Sometimes, the poles repel each other, or push apart.

Do it yourself

Test the force between the poles of two bar magnets.

Tape one of the magnets to a cork and float it on some water. Slowly bring the north pole of the second magnet toward the south pole of the floating magnet to see what happens. Make a chart like the one below and try the other combinations.

Poles	Attract or Repel
south/north	
south/south	
north/north	
north/south	

slice of cork

Magnet Laws

In the experiment below, you've discovered the laws of magnets. A south pole always repels a south pole and a north pole always repels a north pole. But a north pole always attracts a south pole and a south pole always attracts a north pole.

Scientists say:
Like poles repel and unlike poles attract.

Hint: Some magnets have "north" and "south" labeled on them. If your magnets do not have labels, look for a tiny dent at one end. That end is the magnet's north pole.

Do it yourself

Make your own magnets.

Try magnetizing an iron nail and a steel screwdriver. Make them magnetic by stroking them with a magnet at least 50 times. Always stroke the magnet across the nail or screwdriver in one direction only, and lift the magnet away after each stroke.

See how many paper clips the new magnets will pick up.

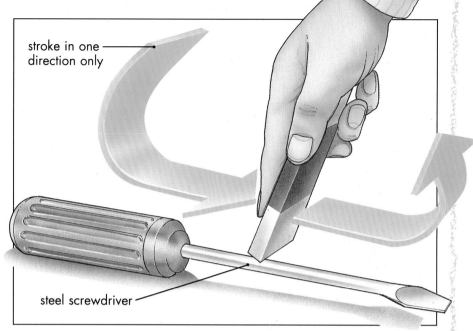

stroke in one direction only

steel screwdriver

How It Works

Iron is made up of lots of tiny magnets that point in different directions. When the iron is magnetized, the tiny magnets all swing around to point in the same direction. This magnetism adds up, making the iron magnetic.

before

after

Steel is made mainly from iron and other things that harden it. The hard steel screwdriver will stay magnetic much longer than the softer iron nail. Try hitting each of them against a stone or rock to see whether they lose any of their magnetism. You will probably find that the iron nail can pick up fewer paper clips than before.

The Pull of the Earth

Did you know that the whole Earth is magnetic? That's why a magnetic compass needle always points in the same direction — the poles of the compass needle are attracted to the Earth's North and South Poles. It's as if the Earth had a huge bar magnet inside. Scientists believe that this magnetism comes from the red-hot melted iron deep inside the Earth.

Getting Home

Homing pigeons can sense the Earth's magnetism. They're able to find their way home after they have been released hundreds of miles away.

Magnetic Flip

Scientists have studied the magnetism in ancient rocks. They've found that every so often the Earth's magnetic North and South Poles swap places. No one knows why this happens, or when it will happen next.

Do it yourself

A compass needle swings freely and always settles down pointing north-south. To make your own compass, you'll need a magnet, a steel needle, a piece of cork, and a shallow dish.

1. Make the needle magnetic in the same way that you magnetized the steel screwdriver (see page 9).

2. Place the needle on the cork and float it in a dish filled with water.

3. When the needle settles down, watch which direction it points in. Check the direction with a real pocket compass and label it North.

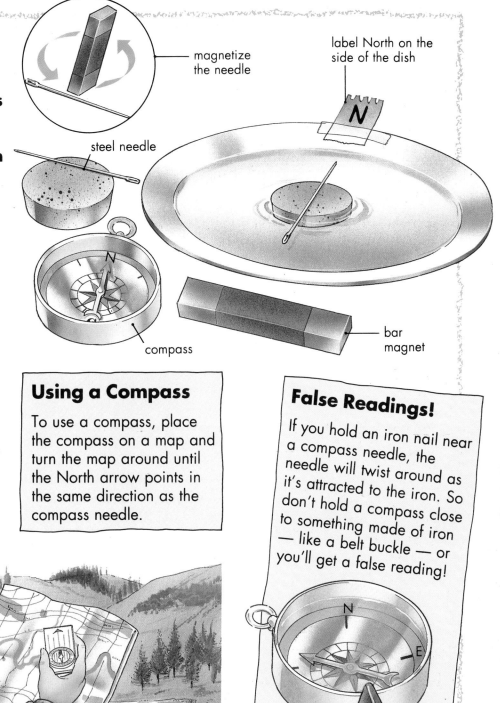

magnetize the needle

steel needle

label North on the side of the dish

N

compass

bar magnet

Using a Compass

To use a compass, place the compass on a map and turn the map around until the North arrow points in the same direction as the compass needle.

False Readings!

If you hold an iron nail near a compass needle, the needle will twist around as it's attracted to the iron. So don't hold a compass close to something made of iron — like a belt buckle — or you'll get a false reading!

N

E

Magnets at Work

Magnets are used to make compasses, and some doors have bar magnets fastened to them to hold them shut. In space, where things do not have any weight, astronauts use magnets to hold things like toothbrushes onto the walls of their spacecraft to stop them floating around. Magnets are also used with electricity to make electric motors work. You can read more about how magnets and electricity are linked on page 24.

A powerful magnet can hold a warning light to the roof of a police car or a doctor's car.

Magnetic Sorting

Food cans are usually made from steel and soda cans from aluminum. The two metals must be separated before they are melted down and recycled. As steel is attracted by magnets and aluminum is not, you can sort them with a magnet.

aluminum — not magnetic

steel — magnetic

Cassette and videotapes use magnetism to record sounds and pictures. The tape is coated with a special magnetic material. Sounds or images are then recorded on to the tape as magnetic patterns.

Do it yourself

Here are ideas for two games you can make using magnets.

bamboo stick

horseshoe magnet

Fish (2 - 6 Players)

Tie small horseshoe magnets to the ends of the bamboo sticks (one for each player). Cut out the plastic fish and write scores on each with a waterproof marker. Attach metal paper clips to the fish. Fill a deep bowl with water and drop in the fish so the numbers are face down.

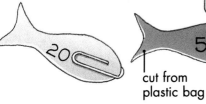

20

5

15

10

cut from plastic bag

metal paper clip

Roundup (2 Players)

Make sheep and sheep pens from cardboard, as shown. Tape a small round magnet to the end of each ruler.

metal paper clip

How To Play Fish

The players should stand at equal distances from the bowl. Shout "Go" and start fishing. At the end of the game, the player with the most points wins.

tray or thin wooden board

small round magnet

tape down

How To Play Roundup

Round up the sheep and put them in your pen. (You can't take sheep out of the other player's pen.) The one with the most sheep wins.

13

Getting Started

The best way to learn about electricity is to experiment with it. But remember — never touch the electricity supply in your home. It can kill.

To get started, collect all the things you'll need and keep them in a box. For some activities, you'll need a buzzer and a motor. You can buy these quite cheaply from a hobby store or an electrical store.

Basic Experiment Kit

1. Batteries (see next page)
2. Balsa wood, or cork pieces
3. Small screwdriver
4. Plastic-coated wire
5. Bulbs and bulb holders
6. Metal paper clips and thumbtacks
7. Tape

Preparing Wire

Most wires come with a plastic coating. To join the wire to a bulb holder or to a paper clip, you must ask an adult to help you strip some of the plastic from the end so you can see the metal. Follow stages 1 to 4 which show you how to do this.

① ② cut ③ pull ④ twist

Wires can also be attached to alligator clips (right) which are then covered with plastic cases.

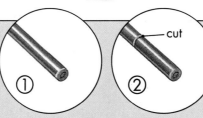

plastic case

alligator clip

Choosing Batteries

All batteries have two terminals — a positive (+) and a negative (–). Look on the outside of your batteries to see how many volts they have.

The simplest batteries are 1.5V (one and a half volts). You can also buy 4.5V or 9V batteries. A 4.5V battery has three 1.5V cells inside it. A 9V battery has six 1.5V cells. Use 1.5V or 4.5V batteries for the experiments in this book.

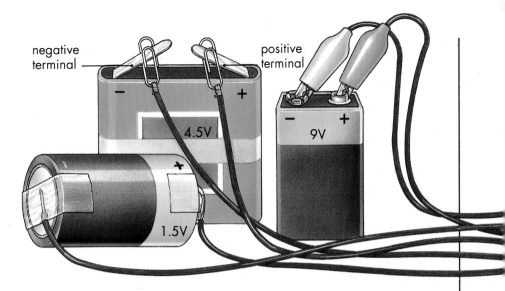

negative terminal

positive terminal

4.5V

9V

1.5V

Join the wires and batteries with tape, metal paper clips, or alligator clips. Or use a battery holder.

Whichever method you use, make sure that the metal parts touch tightly, or your experiments won't work.

battery holder

wind wire tightly around paper clip

Bulbs and Bulb Holders

Bulbs are made to work with a certain number of volts. This number is printed on the base of the bulb. Always use a bulb that is the same number of volts, or more volts, than your battery.

Gently screw the bulb into the holder, then screw the stripped wire under each of the holder's terminals, as shown on the right.

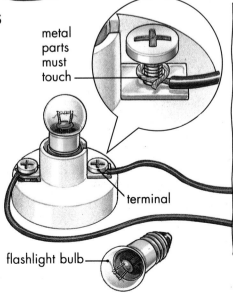

metal parts must touch

terminal

flashlight bulb

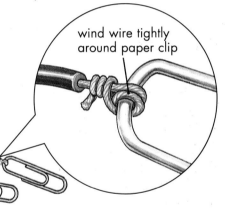

Using LEDs

LEDs (light-emitting diodes) do not need a lot of power to make them light up. Use one for the experiment on page 30.

15

Simple Circuits

To get electricity to light a bulb, it must flow around a complete path, or circuit. The battery provides the power. It pushes an electric current along the wires and through the bulb. An electric circuit works a little like the chain on your bike. When you push the pedals, your power is carried by the chain to the back wheel. If the chain breaks, the wheel won't turn. If an electric circuit is broken, the current stops flowing and the light goes out.

Wires at Work

Connecting the tiny electric circuits in a television is very complicated. Every circuit must be complete or the TV set won't work.

Making a Circuit

Cut two lengths of wire and strip both ends (see page 14). Connect each wire to the battery and bulb holder as shown. You can use tape, paper clips, or alligator clips, as used here.

broken circuit

How It Works

The battery pushes an electric current around the circuit. The current heats the fine wire in the bulb, so it glows.

use alligator clips or wrap wire around the screw

16

Do it yourself

Switches are useful because you can decide whether or not you want the electricity to flow. Make this simple switch to add to your circuit.

1. Take one of the wires off the bulb holder and wrap the end tightly around a thumbtack.

2. Push the tack through the end of a paper clip and into a piece of balsa wood.

balsa wood

first tack

second tack

3. Strip another piece of wire. Connect one end to a second thumbtack and push it into the wood.

4. Connect the free end of the new wire to the free screw on the bulb holder.

5. Light the bulb by turning the paper clip so that it touches both tacks. Move the second thumbtack if the paper clip won't reach.

OFF

ON

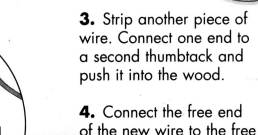

How It Works

When the switch is on, there's a complete circuit for the electricity to flow around, so the bulb lights up. When it's off, there's a break in the circuit, so the electricity can't flow and the bulb won't light.

17

An Electric Test

Materials that carry electricity well are called conductors. Metal is a good conductor of electricity. Things that don't carry electricity are called insulators. Plastic is an insulator. Many electrical wires are covered in plastic, for safety.

Do it yourself

Test a collection of materials to see whether they're conductors or insulators.

1. Take the switch out of your circuit so that you are left with two bare wires. If you touch the two wires together you will complete the circuit and the bulb will glow.

2. Touch the material to be tested with both wires. The bulb will light if the material conducts electricity. A metal nail, for example, will complete the circuit, lighting up the bulb.

3. Make a note of your results.

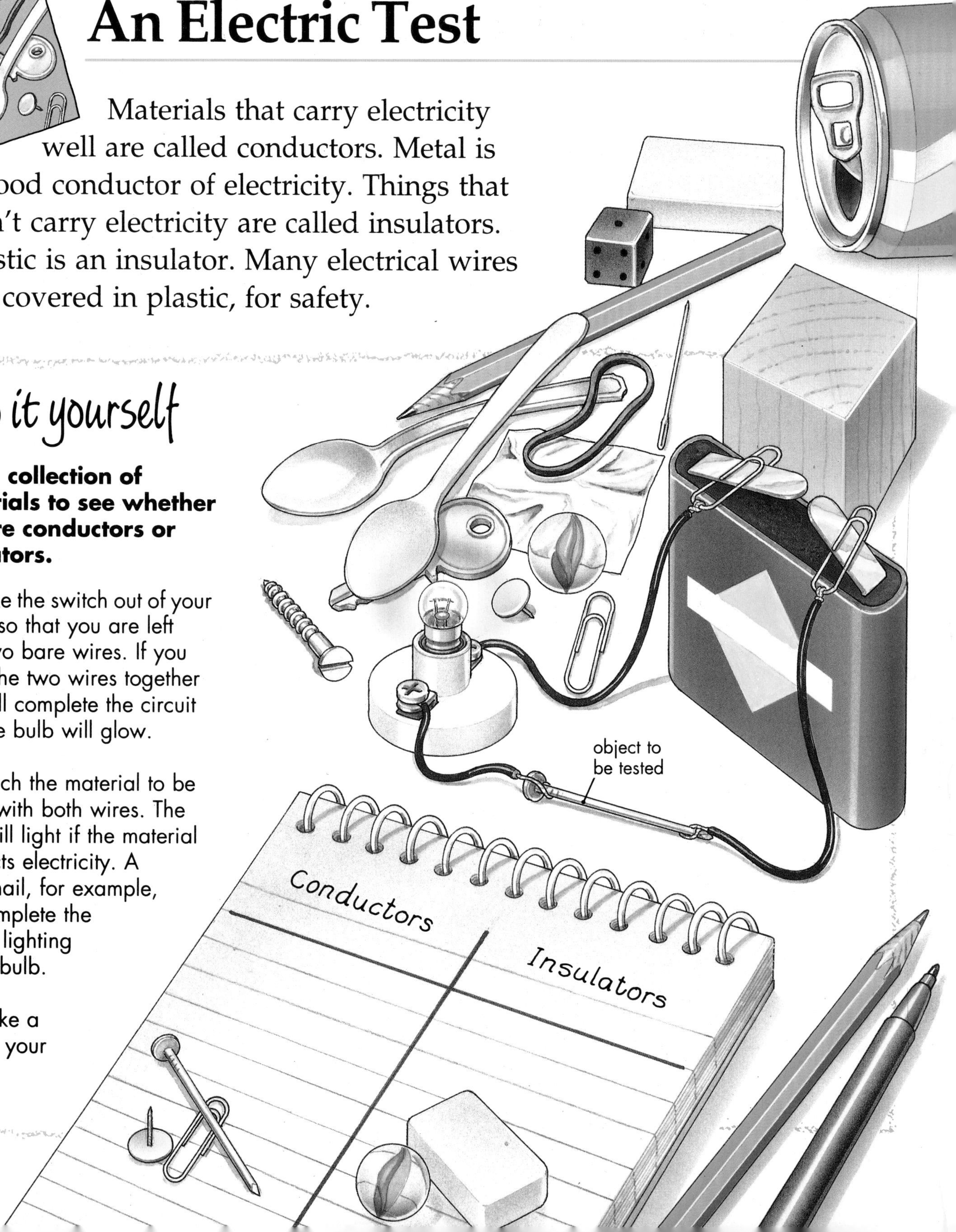

object to be tested

Conductors

Insulators

Three Circuit Projects

Here are three circuit projects for you to try — a burglar alarm, a Morse code key, and a test of skill. For each of the projects you'll need to make a simple circuit and a special sort of switch.

How It Works

When someone steps on them, the two pieces of cardboard touch. As they are wrapped in metal foil, they form a complete circuit, so the buzzer goes off or the bulb lights up.

Do it yourself

To make a burglar alarm, you will need a battery and wires, a buzzer, two plastic straws, aluminum foil, and some cardboard.

1. Cut out two pieces of cardboard. Tape foil around them and make a hole in one end of each piece.

2. Tape the cardboard pieces together with straws in between, so that they are close but do not touch. Attach one wire to each piece of cardboard as shown.

3. Wire your cardboard switch in a circuit with the battery and buzzer. Use long wires so that you can hide your alarm around a corner or even in another room. Use a bulb instead of a buzzer for a silent alarm.

hole

foil

hole

buzzer

hide the switch under a mat

straw

end of foil

straw

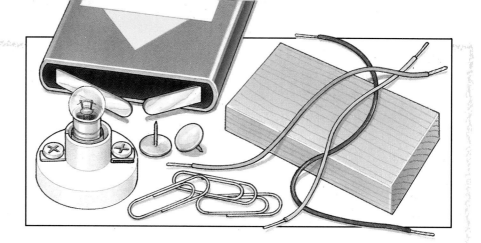

Do it yourself

The first messages sent by electricity were tapped out in a code of dots and dashes called Morse code. Make your own Morse code key.

1. Open out a small paper clip and bend one end up. You can tape a plastic button over the raised end to make it easier to use.

2. Pin the paper clip to a piece of balsa wood with a thumbtack and wire the switch into a circuit. Position the second thumbtack in the balsa wood so that the raised end of the paper clip will touch it.

When you press down the paper clip it will complete the circuit, lighting up the bulb or working the buzzer.

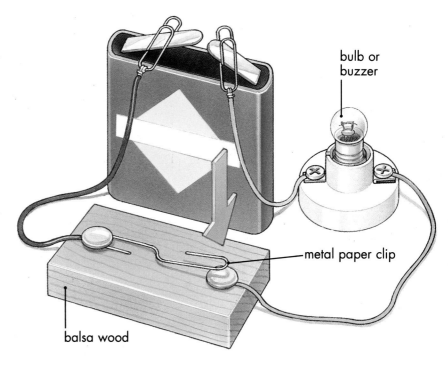

bulb or buzzer

metal paper clip

balsa wood

Morse Code

The International Morse code is shown on the right. Try tapping out messages to your friends. Send a dot by tapping quickly. Send a dash by holding the paper clip down for a little longer.

A ●▬	B ▬●●●	C ▬●▬●
D ▬●●	E ●	F ●●▬●
G ▬▬●	H ●●●●	I ●●
J ●▬▬▬	K ▬●▬	L ●▬●●
M ▬▬	N ▬●	O ▬▬▬
P ●▬▬●	Q ▬▬●▬	R ●▬●
S ●●●	T ▬	U ●●▬
V ●●●▬	W ●▬▬	X ▬●●▬
Y ▬●▬▬	Z ▬▬●●	

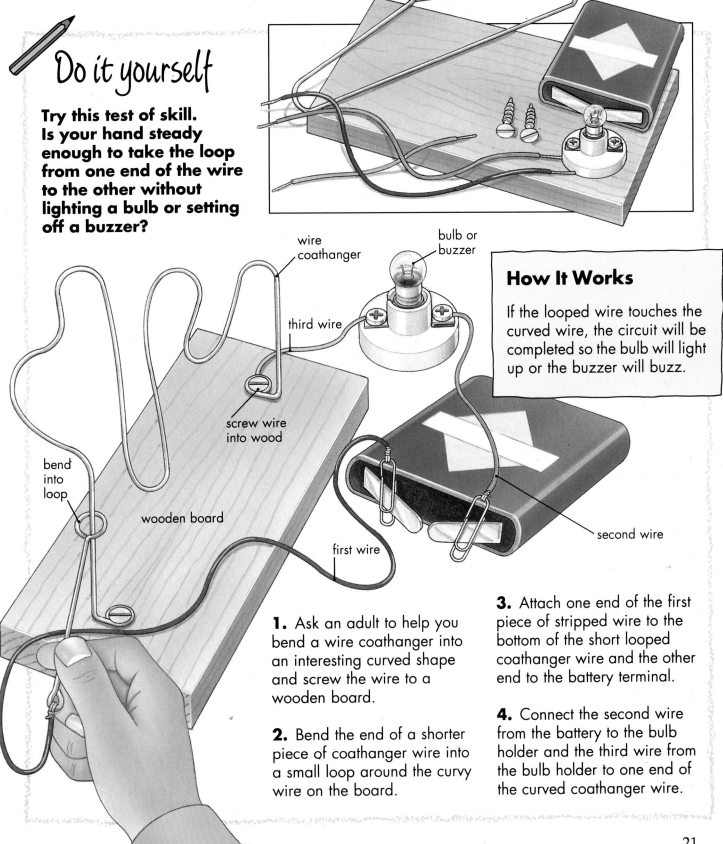

Do it yourself

Try this test of skill. Is your hand steady enough to take the loop from one end of the wire to the other without lighting a bulb or setting off a buzzer?

wire coathanger

bulb or buzzer

third wire

screw wire into wood

bend into loop

wooden board

first wire

second wire

How It Works

If the looped wire touches the curved wire, the circuit will be completed so the bulb will light up or the buzzer will buzz.

1. Ask an adult to help you bend a wire coathanger into an interesting curved shape and screw the wire to a wooden board.

2. Bend the end of a shorter piece of coathanger wire into a small loop around the curvy wire on the board.

3. Attach one end of the first piece of stripped wire to the bottom of the short looped coathanger wire and the other end to the battery terminal.

4. Connect the second wire from the battery to the bulb holder and the third wire from the bulb holder to one end of the curved coathanger wire.

Light at Night

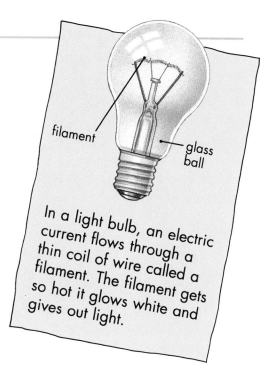

Electric lights have completely changed the way we live. We can do things at night almost as if it were still day. We can play football by floodlight and go shopping in brightly-lit shopping malls. Motorists can drive at night using car headlights, and streetlights show us the road. The centers of some big cities, like Hong Kong below, now have so many lights that astronauts can see them from space.

filament

glass ball

In a light bulb, an electric current flows through a thin coil of wire called a filament. The filament gets so hot it glows white and gives out light.

How Light Bulbs Work

Touch the ends of two wires from a battery to a thread of fine steel wool and see how the wool glows as it is heated. When things burn, they need oxygen gas from the air. Light bulbs don't contain any oxygen, so the filament glows but does not burn away.

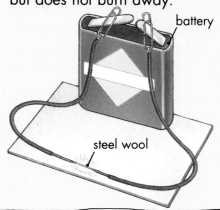

battery

steel wool

Do it yourself

Suppose you want to light two bulbs from just one battery. There are two ways that you can wire up the circuit — as a series circuit or as a parallel circuit.

The two types of circuit are shown below. Wire up both kinds so that you can compare them.

The bulbs in the parallel circuit will glow more brightly than those in the series circuit.

Try taking one of the bulbs out of its holder in each circuit to see what happens to the other bulb.

Eye-Spy

Outdoor Christmas lights are usually wired as a parallel circuit so if one goes out, the rest stay alight. Indoor lights are usually wired as a series circuit, which is safer.

series circuit — bulbs are wired as one single circuit

parallel circuit — bulbs are wired as a double circuit

How It Works

The electricity can only flow one way in a series circuit. If you remove a bulb the circuit will be broken and the other bulb will go out.

In a parallel circuit, each bulb is wired in its own circuit. So if you remove a bulb, the electricity can still flow around the circuit and the other bulb will stay alight.

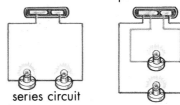

series circuit

parallel circuit

Magnetic Links

In 1820, a scientist called Hans Oersted was experimenting with an electric circuit when he suddenly noticed that a compass needle near the wires moved when he switched the electricity on and off. He had made an important discovery — that an electric current produces magnetism.

In this MAGLEV (magnetic levitation) train, electro-magnets in the train are repelled by magnetism in the track, making the train float along.

Do it yourself

Try repeating Oersted's famous experiment.

1. Wrap a length of wire around a cardboard tube as shown. (This makes the magnetism stronger.) Then connect the wire to a battery and a switch.

2. Slide a small compass into the middle of the tube.

3. Switch the electric circuit on and off and watch what happens to the compass needle.

How It Works

When you switch on the circuit the electricity produces magnetism all around the wire. This attracts the compass needle and makes it swing. When the circuit is off, there is no magnetism produced so the needle goes back to its north-south position.

plastic-coated wire

N

switch is ON

Do it yourself

A magnet that works by electricity is called an electromagnet. Make an electromagnet with a long iron nail, wire, a battery, and a switch.

1. Wind the wire around the nail, as shown. This will become your electromagnet.

2. Wire up the electromagnet in a circuit with the battery and the switch.

3. Switch on the circuit and test the magnet to see if it will pick up paper clips or pins.

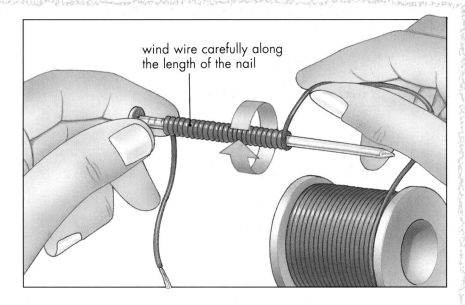

wind wire carefully along the length of the nail

The electric current in the coil of wire makes the tiny magnets inside the iron nail line up, turning the nail itself into a magnet.

More Things to Try

Try bringing one end of the electromagnet toward a compass needle to see whether the needle is attracted or repelled. Then try the same thing with the other end of the magnet.

Now change the wires around on your battery and try the same thing again. Your results should now be the other way around.

electromagnet

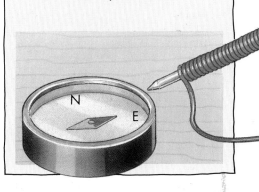

25

Electric Sounds

When you play a cassette tape or listen to the radio, you are hearing sounds that have been made with electricity. Buzzers, bells, and loudspeakers also turn electricity into sound.

Telephones work in a similar way. They change the sounds of our voices into electricity. These electric signals can be carried along wires to another phone, or beamed by satellite to the other side of the world.

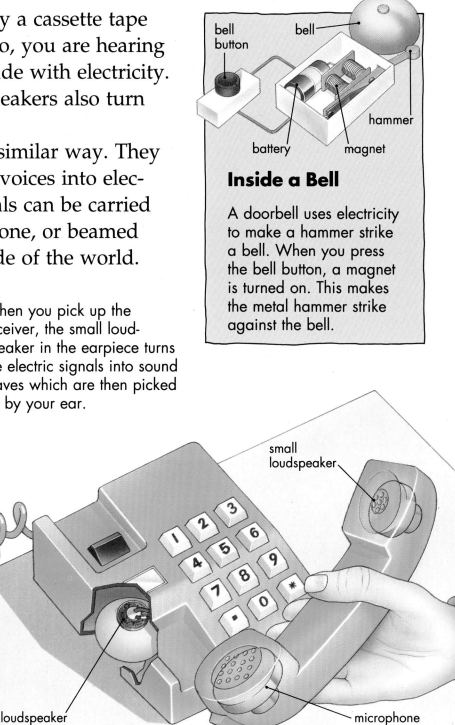

bell button **bell** **hammer** **battery** **magnet**

Inside a Bell

A doorbell uses electricity to make a hammer strike a bell. When you press the bell button, a magnet is turned on. This makes the metal hammer strike against the bell.

When you pick up the receiver, the small loudspeaker in the earpiece turns the electric signals into sound waves which are then picked up by your ear.

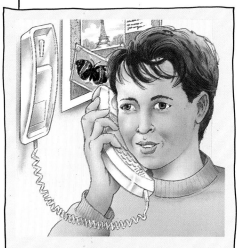

First Telephone Call

Imagine life without telephones! Alexander Graham Bell invented the telephone in 1876. The first words he spoke were to his assistant. He said, "Mr. Watson, come here, I want you."

small loudspeaker

loudspeaker

microphone

Do it yourself

Discover how electric signals are turned back into sounds. You'll need an old transistor radio earpiece or loudspeaker, and a battery.

The wires of old radio ear-pieces usually have two strands. Carefully separate the strands and touch the end of one strand to one battery terminal and the end of the other strand to the other battery terminal. What do you hear?

If you have one, try this same experiment with an old radio loudspeaker. You should be able to see and feel the loudspeaker cone move slightly when the battery is connected.

An earpiece also makes a good *static* electricity detector. Try rubbing a balloon with some wool and then touch the balloon with the ear-piece wires.

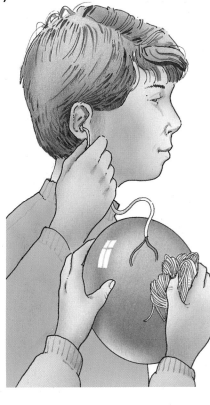

Inside a Loudspeaker

In a radio, it's the loudspeaker that makes sounds. Inside, there's a magnet and a coil of wire. When an electric current flows through the coil, it's pushed back and forth by the magnet. The coil makes the cone move backward and forward too, producing sounds.

wire coil

cone

Electric Motors

Another important discovery to do with electricity and magnetism was made in 1821 by a scientist called Michael Faraday. He found out that magnetism from an electric current can be used to make electric motors turn.

Compared to gasoline engines, electric motors are clean and quiet. It's possible that in the future we may have electric cars which could help to keep our cities cleaner and cause less pollution.

Eye-Spy

Look out for things around your home that use electric motors. (Don't turn anything on without asking first.)

drill

razor

hairdryer

Turning Motors

Buy a cheap electric motor from a hobby store to try this experiment. Attach a block from a construction kit to the motor's spindle so you can see which way the motor turns.

Connect the motor to some batteries. See which way the motor turns and how fast it goes. Now try connecting the wires the other way around. The spindle should now turn in the opposite direction.

electric motor

batteries

battery holder

spindle

metal or plastic block from a construction kit

Do it yourself

Try building this electric winch.

1. Ask an adult to help you cut three pieces of wood to the shapes shown on the right and nail them together.

2. Slide two empty spools onto a dowel and glue them together. Make sure that the spools can turn freely.

3. Hook a rubber band over one of the spools and slide the dowel through the holes in the side pieces. Then glue the dowel firmly in place.

4. Attach the electric motor to the base board with tape.

5. Connect the motor to a battery and switch.

6. Glue the end of a piece of string to the second spool and wind the string around it several times. Attach a load to the free end of the string.

When you turn on the switch, the motor should turn the spools, winding in the string and load.

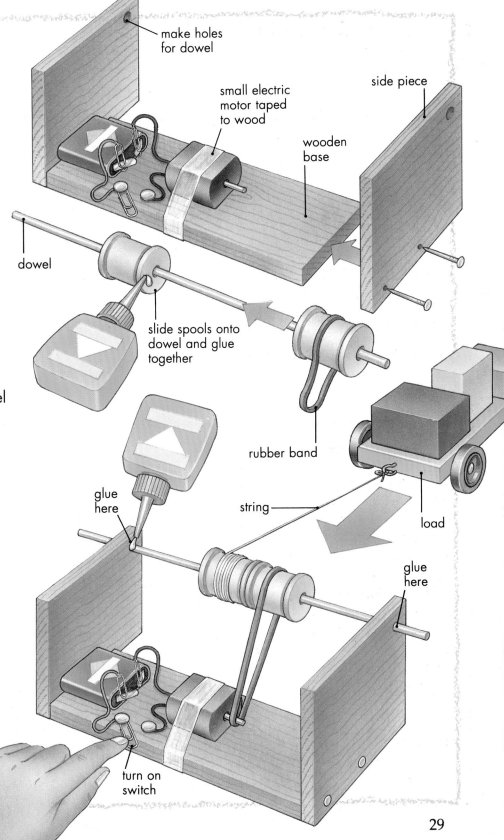

make holes for dowel

small electric motor taped to wood

side piece

wooden base

dowel

slide spools onto dowel and glue together

rubber band

glue here

string

load

glue here

turn on switch

29

Making Currents

Did you know that there is electricity in almost everything, but it only flows when it is given energy or power? This energy can come from the chemicals in a battery, from moving magnets, or from sunlight falling on a solar cell.

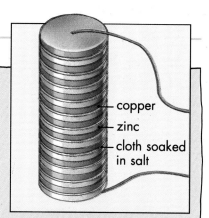

- copper
- zinc
- cloth soaked in salt

The First Battery

The first battery was made by Alessandro Volta in 1800. Volta discovered that when copper and zinc are stacked alternately and separated by strips of cloth soaked in salty water or an acid, an electric current flows between them.

Do it yourself

Try making a simple battery with vinegar.

1. Fill three small glass jars with vinegar (an acid).

2. Wrap bare copper wire around two galvanized (zinc-coated) nails, and link jars 1 and 2, and 2 and 3 as shown.

3. Put a third nail in jar 3 and a third piece of wire in jar 1. These are your battery's terminals.

4. Connect the terminals to an LED and you should see it light up.

copper wire

galvanized nail

vinegar

2

1

3

LED (light-emitting diode)

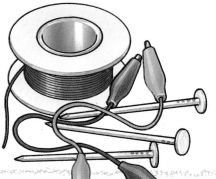

Solar Power

Solar cells turn light from the Sun into electricity. Many pocket calculators are powered by sunlight. There have also been experiments with solar-powered cars (right) and planes, but they need a sunny climate to work well. Solar-powered machines do not cause pollution.

Moving Magnets

Some bicycle lamps use a simple dynamo to make an electric current. The turning wheel moves a magnet inside a wire coil, making the light come on. Today, most bicycle lamps work with batteries.

dynamo

Animal Electricity

Some fish can make their own electric currents. Catfish use electricity to feel their way along the bottom of a stream or river. Electric eels stun their prey with an electric shock — they can produce an electric shock that is powerful enough to knock down a person.

31

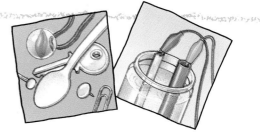

Index

alligator clips 14, 16, 19, 23, 30

batteries 14, 16, 30
   choosing 15
battery holder 15, 28
Bell, Alexander Graham 26
bulb holder 15
bulbs, choosing 16
burglar alarm 19
buzzer 14, 19, 20, 21, 26

circuit 16
   parallel 23
   series 23
compass 10, 11, 12, 24, 25
conductor 18
current electricity 4

dynamo 31

Earth, the 8, 10
electric eel 31
electromagnet 24, 25

Faraday, Michael 28
filament 22

insulator 18
iron 6, 8, 9, 10, 11
iron filings 6, 7

LED 15, 30
light bulb 14, 15, 22
lightning 5
lodestone 6
loudspeaker 26, 27

MAGLEV train 24
magnetic flip 10
magnetic tape 12, 26
magnetite 6
magnets, laws of 8
Morse code 20
Morse, Samuel 20
motor, electric 12, 14, 28

North Pole 8, 10

Oersted, Hans 24

parallel circuit 23
poles, of magnets 7, 8

satellite 26
series circuit 23
solar power 30, 31
South Pole 8, 10
static electricity 4, 5, 27
steel 9, 11, 12
steel wool 22
switches, making 17

telephone 26
television 4, 16
terminal 15
test of skill 21

volt 15, 30
Volta, Alessandro 30

winch, electric 29
wires, preparing 14